DISCOVERING LANGUAGES
SPANISH

REVISED EDITION

Elaine S. Robbins

Formerly Mount Logan Middle School
Logan, Utah

Kathryn R. Ashworth

Brigham Young University

AMSCO SCHOOL PUBLICATIONS, INC.
315 Hudson Street / New York, N.Y. 10013

To the memory of

Carl C. Robbins Jr., beloved son and brother of the authors

When ordering this book, please specify R 594 S
or DISCOVERING LANGUAGES: SPANISH

Revised Edition

Design and Production: Boultinghouse & Boultinghouse, Inc.

Cover Illustration: Delana Bettoli

Illustrations: Rick Brown, John R. Jones, Elise Mills, Ed Taber, George Ulrick

ISBN 978-1-56765-491-2

NYC Item 56765-491-1

10   08

To the Student

You are about to embark on a journey of discovery — beginning to learn a new language spoken by millions of people around the world, SPANISH.

Learning Spanish provides an opportunity to explore another language and culture. Spanish may be one of several languages you will discover in this course. You can then select which language you will continue to study.

Whatever your goals, this book will be a fun beginning in exploring a special gift you have as a human being: the ability to speak a language other than your own. The more you learn how to communicate with other people, the better you will be able to live and work in the world around you.

In this book, you will discover the Spanish language and the world where it is spoken. The Spanish words and expressions you will learn have been limited so that you will feel at ease.

You will learn how to express many things in Spanish: how to greet people, how to count, how to tell the day and month of the year, how to identify and describe many objects, and more.

You will use Spanish to talk about yourself and your friends. You will practice with many different activities, like puzzles and word games, Spanish songs, cartoons, and pictures. Some activities you will do with classmates or with the whole class. You will act out skits and conversations and sing Spanish songs. You will learn about many interesting bits of Spanish culture: school days, holidays, leisure time, sports, families and interesting manners and customs.

You will also meet young Rosita,* who will be your guide on how to pronounce Spanish words. Look for Rosita's clues throughout this book and get a feel for the Spanish language, its sounds, and its musical quality. You will also develop an ear for Spanish, so listen carefully to your teacher and the cassettes.

You will quickly realize that learning a new language is not as hard as you might have imagined. Enjoy using it with your teacher and classmates. Try not to be shy or afraid of making mistakes when speaking: remember, the more you speak, the more you will learn. And you can even show off the Spanish you learn to family, relatives, and friends. After all, learning a new language means talking with the rest of the world and with each other.

Now — on to Spanish. **¡Buena suerte!**, which means *Good luck!*

— *K.R.A.*

* Note that on the cassette the part of Rosita is played by her twin sister Conchita.

Contents

Spain, Spanish America, and the Spanish Language

1

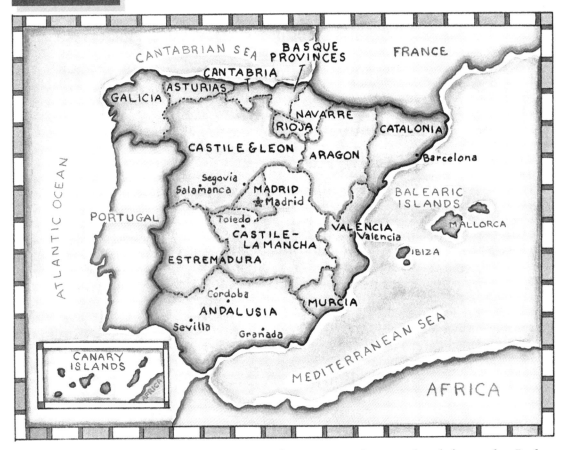

Spanish is one of the major Romance languages that evolved from the Indo-European family of languages. It is the language of 380 million people in 21 countries and the fourth most widely spoken language in the world. Although these Spanish-speaking countries share a common language, they are different from one another: each has its own form of government, economic system, monetary currency, customs, and traditions particular to its people and history.

Spanish is the official language of Spain, including the Canary and the Balearic Islands.

Spain, slightly smaller than the state of Texas, has 40 million inhabitants. Situated at the western edge of the European continent, Spain borders on France to the northeast and Portugal to the west. Three of its sides border on water: the Mediterranean Sea, the Cantabrian Sea, and the Atlantic Ocean.

Most Spanish words derive from Latin, but many words are of Arabic origin as a consequence of the Moorish occupation of Spain from the eighth to the fifteenth centuries. This period, lasting seven centuries and sometimes called the Reconquest, was marked by conflict and wars between the Moors and the Christians of the Spanish kingdoms. The Reconquest proved to be such a long struggle because the various Spanish kingdoms were not united and each fought for its own interests and territory. Finally, in 1492, King Ferdinand and Queen Isabella completed the reconquest of the Spanish kingdoms, expelled the Moors, and for the first time united Christian Spain as a country. 1492 was also the year the King and Queen sponsored Christopher Columbus's expedition to the Americas.

By the 1500s, Spain had become a major world power. With its mighty fleet, Spain began her great exploration and colonization of Central and South America. Spanish became the dominant language of the territories settled by the Spaniards. Today, Spanish is the official language of more than 240 million people living in what may be called Spanish America, which includes Mexico and eighteen countries located in Central America, South America, and the Caribbean.

There are also 22 million Spanish-speaking people in the United States, giving the U.S. the fourth largest Spanish-speaking population in the world. In some American cities in Texas, New Mexico, Arizona, California, New York, and Florida, the concentration of Spanish speakers is so high that Hispanics represent more than half the population. Most Americans of Hispanic origin came from Mexico, Cuba, and Puerto Rico, although there are also large numbers of immigrants from the Dominican Republic, Colombia, and Nicaragua.

CARIBBEAN SEA

Caracas
VENEZUELA

*Bogotá
COLOMBIA

Quito*
ECUADOR

PERU

S O U T H   A M E R I C A

★ Lima

BOLIVIA
★ La Paz

PARAGUAY

CHILE

★ Asunción

ARGENTINA

URUGUAY

Santiago ★

Buenos Aires ★ ★ Montevideo

PACIFIC OCEAN

ATLANTIC OCEAN

Many civilizations flourished in Spanish America before the arrival of the Spaniards in the fifteenth century, primarily the Maya, Aztec, and Inca. Ruins in Mexico, Guatemala, and Peru attest to the greatness and ingenuity of these peoples, who left a rich testament of their artistic accomplishments in architecture, sculpture, murals, and jewelry.

In the fifteenth century, the region of **Castilla** was the most powerful of the Spanish kingdoms: its language, Castilian, became the official language of the country. Although Castilian Spanish is still the official language of Spain, Spaniards of certain regions of Spain also speak different regional languages or dialects, such as **catalán, gallego,** and **vascuense,** an ancient language unrelated to any other on earth.

The Spaniards who settled in Spanish America came mostly from a region in southern Spain called **Andalucía.** They brought to the lands they settled what may be called *Andalusian* Spanish. The main difference between Castilian and Andalusian Spanish is the pronunciation of **c** (before **e** or **i**) and the **z** sound. In Castilian, the **c** of **cero** and the **z** of **zebra** are both pronounced like *th.* In Andalusian, the letters **c** and **z** are both pronounced with the *s* sound.

There are 26 letters in the Spanish alphabet. The letters **k** and **w** do not exist in Spanish, although they may be found in words borrowed from other languages. The Spanish alphabet contains the additional letters **ch, ñ, ll,** and **rr.** When a sentence ends with a ? or !, it begins with ¿ or ¡.

In the same way that American English words and expressions have changed from British English (**lift** = *elevator*, **flat** = *apartment*), so the Spanish spoken in different parts of the world has differing vocabulary. For example, a Puerto Rican ordering a **china** (*orange*) in Spain would not be understood by a Spaniard, who calls an orange a **naranja**. A **papa** (*potato*) in Mexico is called a **patata** in Spain.

Food also varies from country to country in the Spanish-speaking world. You are probably most familiar with dishes from Mexico. **Tacos**, **tamales**, **enchiladas**, and **burritos** all originated in Mexico. They are all rich in beans and corn, crops grown by those who inhabited Mexico before Columbus. From Hispanic countries in the Caribbean come **tostones** (*fried green plantains*) and **empanadillas** (*meat-filled turnovers*). Pork and seafood, beans, corn, and potatoes are important ingredients of Hispanic cooking (in the Andes there are more than thirty varieties of potatoes). A favorite Spanish dish is **paella,** a combination of rice, seafood, chicken, and sausages served with vegetables and spices.

The great tradition of Spanish literature continues to influence contemporary writers. Perhaps you have seen pictures of a tall, skinny knight battling windmills. He is Don Quijote, a creation of the writer Miguel de Cervantes, who lived in sixteenth-century Spain. Don Quijote rode Rocinante, a broken-down horse, and traveled with his short, fat friend, Sancho Panza, as they searched for adventure.

In the twentieth century, many Hispanic novelists have reached international acclaim, among them Jorge Borges, Octavio Paz, Gabriel García Márquez, Pablo Neruda, and Carlos Feuntes. Also of the twentieth century, three outstanding Spanish painters are Pablo Picasso, Salvador Dalí, and Joan Miró. Many of their paintings hang in the Prado, a beautiful art museum in Madrid, Spain.

Spanish-speaking countries also have many popular art forms. Music, for example, is a rich component of everyday life in Spain and Spanish America. Much of the popular music is based on traditional and folkloristic themes. Perhaps you have heard some of the exciting rhythms from the Spanish-speaking world: mariachi music from Mexico, the rumba, merengue, and mambo from the Caribbean, the tango from Argentina, and flamenco from Spain and Spanish America.

Fiestas or popular festivals are also a Spanish tradition very much alive in Spain and Hispanic countries. Each region, no matter how small, has its own festival, celebrated in honor of a saint for whom the town feels a particular devotion. These festivals include parades, lively music, and dancing in the streets, where tempting food specialties of the region may be sampled at every corner. Another type of festival, also considered a sport, is the bullfight. It is popular not only in Spain but also in other Hispanic countries. The tradition of bullfighting can be traced back to very ancient times.

Now — on to the study of this beautiful and influential language. Have fun and enjoy it!

1. Who sponsored Christopher Columbus's expedition to the Americas?

_____

2. Why is Spanish spoken in Central and South America? _____

_____

3. Look at the map on page 4 and name the Spanish-speaking countries of

Central America and the Caribbean. _____

_____

4. Which continent has the greatest number of Spanish-speaking countries?

_____

5. Which country has the fourth largest Spanish-speaking population?

_____

6. Name three civilizations that flourished in Spanish America before the

fifteenth century. _____

7. Name three regional languages or dialects spoken in Spain.

_____

8. How do you pronounce the letters **c** and **z** in Castilian Spanish?

_____

9. How many letters does the Spanish alphabet contain? _____

10. What is **paella**? _____

11. Who is Don Quijote? _____

12. Name three twentieth-century Spanish painters. _____

_____

2 *Spanish Cognates*

You already know many Spanish words. Some of the words are spelled exactly like English words. In many other words, the only difference between Spanish and English is one or two letters. Here are some clues to watch for. Spanish **f** is equivalent to English *ph*: **foto** = *photo*, **teléfono** = *telephone*; words ending in -**ción** in Spanish often end in -*tion* in English: **generación** = *generation*, **internacional** = *international*; words ending in -**dad** in Spanish frequently end in -*ty* in English: **realidad** = *reality*, **actividad** = *activity*. You will also find words like **automóvil**, where Spanish **v** is replaced by English *b*. In Spanish, the letters **b** and **v** are both pronounced like a soft *b*.

How many of the following Spanish words can you recognize? Fill in the blanks with the English meanings. If you need to, you may look in a dictionary. Listen to your teacher or the cassette for the pronunciation of these words:

1. actriz _____

2. aire _____

3. arte _____

4. artista _____

5. automóvil _____

6. banco _____

7. béisbol _____

8. bicicleta _____

9. calculadora _____

10. canoa _____

11. chocolate _____

12. científico _____

13. clase _____

14. concierto _____

15. crema _____

16. delicioso _____

17. dentista _____

18. diferente _____

19. Europa _____

20. excelente _____

21. fabuloso _____

22. familia _____

23. fantástico _____

24. favorito _____

25. foto _____

26. fruta _____

27. generación _____

28. geografía _____

29. globo _____

30. gorila _____

31. grupo _____

32. guitarra _____

33. hamburguesa _____

34. huracán _____

35. importante _____

36. independiente _____

37. internacional _____

38. laboratorio _____

39. mapa _____

40. matemáticas _____

41. norte

42. oficina _____

43. piloto _____

44. posible _____

45. teléfono _____

46. tigre _____

47. tomate _____

48. tren _____

49. trompeta _____

50. volibol _____

3 *Spanish Names*

Now that you are able to recognize over 50 Spanish words resembling English, let's look at how Spanish and English names compare.

Rosita is going to help you learn how to pronounce some of these names.

You will meet **Rosita** throughout this book holding her lens over one or two pronunciation clues she wants to share with you as you develop a good Spanish pronunciation.

Whenever you look at **Rosita**'s clues, keep this in mind: every time you try to pronounce a Spanish sound, hold your mouth, tongue, lips, and teeth in the same position at the end of the sound as you did at the beginning. Try saying **o** this way. Now try **oooo**. There, you've got it.

Rosita has two clues for you before you listen to the following list of boys' and girls' names. These clues will tell you how to pronounce HER name:

Rosita

a = a in ah!

o = o in row

Alfonso, Carlos

Here is a list of boys' and girls' names. With your teacher's help, choose a Spanish name that you would like to have for yourself while you are studying Spanish:

Alberto	Felipe	Gabriel	Jaime	Julio
Alejandro	Fernando	Gilberto	José (Pepe)	Lorenzo
Alfonso	Francisco (Paco)	Guillermo	Juan	Luis
Andrés				Manuel
Antonio				Marcos
Benjamín				Miguel
Carlos				Nicolás
Claudio				Pablo
David				Pedro
Diego				Rafael
Eduardo				Ramón
Enrique				Ricardo
Ernesto				Roberto
Esteban				Tomás
Federico				Víctor

Adela	Emilia	Gloria	Isabel	Laura
Alberta	Estela	Inés	Josefina	Leonor
Alicia	Eva	Irene	Juana	Lucía
Ana María				Luisa
Ana				Magdalena
Bárbara				Margarita
Beatriz				María
Carlota				(Mariucha)
Carmen				Patricia
Carolina				Rosalía
Catalina				Sara
Cecilia				Sofía
Dolores				Susana
Elena				Teresa
Elisa				Virginia

When Spanish speakers want to say, "My name is Pilar," they say, **"Me llamo Pilar."** Practice telling your teacher and your classmates your name in Spanish. If you and your teacher have chosen Spanish names, use them.

Rosita's clues:

Elisa, Jaime

artista, volibol

mucho gusto

* **Tú** means *you* in Spanish; **tú** is used when you are speaking to a close relative, a friend, or a child—someone with whom you are familiar. To say *you*, the Spanish also use **usted** when speaking to a stranger or a grown-up—a person with whom you should be formal. The exercises in this book use **tú** and its related form **te**.

Now let's review what you learned in Dialog 1:

1. Buenos días, _____ (name).

Buenos días, _____ (name).

2. ¿Cómo te llamas?

Me llamo _____.

3. Mucho gusto, _____ (name).

El gusto es mío, _____ (name).

4. Adiós.
Adiós.

Rincón cultural

Spanish Names

Hispanic children are very lucky: they celebrate not only their birthday but also their name day, known in Spanish as **el Día del Santo** because most Spanish names come from the names of saints. If you look at a Spanish calendar you will notice that each day is devoted to a different saint. On their name day, Hispanic children may receive presents and celebrate at a party with relatives and friends. Everyone wishes them **¡Feliz día de tu santo!** (*Happy Name Day!*)

Spanish names are, of course, different from American names. Each person has two family names: the father's last name followed by the mother's maiden name. For example, if a girl's full name is **Ana Gómez Álvarez**, it means that her father's last

ENERO
1	María Madre de D.
2	S. Gregorio N.
3	Sta. Genoveva
4	Sta. Mónica
5	S. Eufrasio
6	**EPIFANÍA**
7	S. Raimundo de P.
8	S. Severino
9	S. Julián
10	S. Nicanor
11	S. Martín de L.
12	Sta. Tatiana
13	S. Hilario
14	S. Fulgencio
15	S. Pablo p. e.
16	S. Marino
17	S. Antonio de E.
18	Sta. Vicenta
19	S. Mario
20	S. Sebastián
21	Sta. Inés
22	S. Vicente
23	S. Ildefonso
24	S. Francisco de S.
25	Conv. de S. Pablo
26	S. Timoteo
27	Sta. Angela de M.
28	Sto. Tomás de A.
29	S. Pedro N.
30	S. Lesmes
31	S. Juan Bosco

FEBRERO
1	Sta. Brígida
2	**Pres. del Señor**
3	S. Oscar
4	S. Juan de B.
5	Sta. Águeda
6	S. Pablo Miki
7	S. Romualdo
8	S. Jerónimo E.
9	Sta. Apolonia
10	Sta. Escolástica
11	Sra. de Lourdes
12	Sta. Eulalia
13	S. Benigno
14	S. Metodio
15	S. Claudio
16	S. Onésimo
17	Siete Santos
18	S. Eladio
19	S. Conrado
20	Sta. Amanda
21	S. Pedro D.
22	S. Pedro
23	S. Policarpo
24	S. Modesto
25	S. Cesáreo
26	S. Alejandro
27	S. Leandro
28	S. Gabriel de D.

MARZO
1	S. Albino
2	S. Heraclio
3	S. Juan de D.
4	S. Casimiro
5	S. Adrián
6	S. Olegario
7	Sta. Felícitas
8	S. Juan
9	Sta. Francisca R.
10	S. Cavo
11	S. Eulogio
12	S. Gregorio M.
13	S. Rodrigo
14	Sta. Matilde
15	S. Raimundo de F.
16	S. Ciriaco
17	S. Patricio
18	S. Cirilo de J.
19	S. José
20	S. Martín de D.
21	S. Alfonso de R.
22	S. Bienvenido
23	S. Toribio de M.
24	S. Agapito
25	**ANUNCIACIÓN**
26	S. Braulio
27	S. Ruperto
28	Sta. Gundelina
29	Sta. Beatriz de S.
30	S. Juan Cl.
31	S. Benjamín

ABRIL
1	S. Hugo
2	S. Francisco de P.
3	S. Ricardo
4	S. Isodoro
5	S. Vicente F.
6	Sta. Juliana
7	S. Juan Bautista
8	S. Dionisio
9	Sta. Casilda
10	S. Miguel de los S.
11	S. Estanislao
12	S. Víctor
13	S. Martín I.
14	S. Tiburcio
15	S. Telmo
16	Sta. Engracia
17	Sta. Clara
18	S. Perfecto
19	S. Hermógenes
20	S. Teodoro
21	S. Anselmo
22	S. Lucio
23	S. Jorge
24	S. Fidel
25	S. Marcos
26	Ntra. Sra. del B.
27	Sta. Zita
28	S. Pedro Ch.
29	Sta. Catalina de S.
30	S. Pío V.

MAYO
1	S. José O.
2	S. Atanasio
3	S. Felipe
4	S. Silvano
5	S. Máximo
6	S. Heliodoro
7	Sta. Flavia
8	S. Víctor
9	S. Gregorio O.
10	San Juan de A.
11	S. Francisco J.
12	S. Nereo
13	S. Miguel G.
14	S. Matías
15	S. Isidro
16	Sta. Felicia
17	S. Pascual
18	S. Juan I.
19	S. Juan de C.
20	S. Bernardino
21	S. Andrés B.
22	Sta. Rita
23	S. Desiderio
24	**María Auxiliadora**
25	S. Gregorio VII
26	S. Felipe N.
27	S. Agustín de C.
28	S. Justo
29	S. Félix
30	S. Fernando
31	**Visit. de la Virgen**

JUNIO
1	S. Justino
2	S. Marcelino
3	S. Carlos L.
4	S. Francisco
5	S. Bonifacio
6	S. Norberto
7	S. Pedro de C.
8	S. Eutropio
9	S. Efrén
10	S. Aresio
11	S. Bernabé
12	S. Juan de S.
13	S. Antonio de P.
14	S. Basilio
15	S. Benilde
16	S. Juan F.
17	Sta. Sancha
18	S. Venancio
19	Sta. Juliana
20	Sta. Florentina
21	S. Luis G.
22	S. Paulino
23	S. Áñigo
24	Nat. S. Juan B.
25	S. Guillermo
26	S. Marciano
27	S. Cirilo de A.
28	S. Ireneo
29	S. Pedro y Pablo
30	S. Marcial

JULIO
1	S. Simeón
2	S. Vidal
3	Sto. Tomás
4	Sta. Isabel de P.
5	S. Antonio M. Z.
6	Sta. María G.
7	S. Fermín
8	S. Edgar
9	Sta. Verónica
10	S. Honorato
11	S. Benito
12	S. Juan G.
13	S. Enrique
14	S. Camilo
15	S. Buenaventura
16	Ntra. Sra. del Carmen
17	S. Mártires del B.
18	S. Federico
19	Sta. Áurea
20	S. Pablo de C.
21	S. Lorenzo
22	Sta. María Magd.
23	Sta. Brígida
24	S. Francisco S.
25	S. Santiago
26	S. Joaquín
27	S. Aurelio
28	S. Gerardino
29	Sta. Marta
30	S. Pedro Cr.
31	S. Ignacio de L.

AGOSTO
1	S. Alfonso M.
2	S. Eusebio
3	S. Lidia
4	S. Juan María
5	Sta. María la Mayor
6	Transf. del Señor
7	Sto. Domingo
8	S. Cayetano
9	S. Marcelino
10	S. Lorenzo
11	Sta. Clara
12	S. Graciliano
13	S. Ponciano
14	S. Ursicio
15	**ASUNCIÓN**
16	S. Esteban de H.
17	S. Jacinto
18	Sta. Elena
19	S. Juan E.
20	S. Bernardo
21	S. Pío X
22	Sta. María Reina
23	Sta. Rosa
24	S. Bartolomé
25	S. Luis de Fr.
26	Sta. María Micaela
27	Sta. Mónica
28	S. Agustín
29	S. Juan Bautista
30	S. Esteban de Z.
31	S. Ramón

SEPTIEMBRE
1	S. Gil
2	S. Antolín
3	S. Gregorio
4	Sta. Cándida
5	S. Sancho
6	S. Juan de R.
7	Sta. Regina
8	**Nativ. de María**
9	S. Pedro C.
10	S. Nicolás de T.
11	Sta. Teodora
12	S. Leoncio
13	S. Juan Cr.
14	**Exaltac. Santa Cruz**
15	Virgen de los Dolor.
16	S. Cornelio
17	S. Roberto
18	S. José de C.
19	S. Jenaro
20	Sta. Imelda
21	S. Mateo
22	S. Mauricio
23	S. Constancio
24	Sta. Mercedes
25	S. Cleofás
26	S. Damián
27	S. Daniel
28	S. Wenceslao
29	S. Rafael
30	S. Jerónimo

OCTUBRE
1	Sta. Teresita
2	S. Angeles C.
3	S. Virilio
4	S. Francisco de A.
5	S. Froilán
6	S. Bruno
7	Ntra. Sra. del Ros.
8	S. Juan de Jesus
9	S. Luis B.
10	Ntra. Sra. del Pil.
11	Sta. Soledad
12	Sta. Serafín
13	S. Eduardo
14	S. Calixto
15	Sta. Teresa
16	Sta. Margarita de P.
17	S. Ignacio de A.
18	S. Lucas
19	S. Pedro de A.
20	Sta. Irene
21	S. Hilarión
22	Sta. Nunila
23	S. Juan de C.
24	S. Antonio
25	S. Crisanto
26	S. Felicísimo
27	S. Florencio
28	S. Simón
29	S. Narciso
30	S. Alonso
31	S. Quintín

NOVIEMBRE
1	**Todos los Santos**
2	**Fieles Difuntos**
3	S. Martín de P.
4	S. Carlos B.
5	S. Galación
6	S. Leonardo
7	S. Amaranto
8	S. Godofeo
9	S. Alejandro
10	S. León
11	S. José K.
12	Cuatro Santos
13	S. Eugenio
14	S. Gerardo
15	Sta. Eugenia
16	Sta. Gertrudis
17	Sta. Isabel de H.
18	S. Pedro y Pablo
19	S. Crispín
20	S. Félix de V.
21	**Pres. de la Virgen**
22	Sta. Cecilia
23	S. Clemente
24	Sta. Flora
25	S. Erasmo
26	S. Leonardo
27	S. Alberto
28	S. Jaime
29	S. Saturnino
30	S. Andrés

DICIEMBRE
1	S. Eloy
2	Sta. Bibiana
3	S. Francisco J.
4	S. Juan D.
5	S. Humberto
6	S. Nicolás
7	S. Ambrosio
8	**Imm. Concepción**
9	Sta. Valeria
10	Imm. Concepción Eulalia
11	S. Daniel
12	Sta. Juana F.
13	Sta. Lucía
14	S. Juan de la C.
15	Sta. Silvia
16	S. Adón
17	S. Roque
18	Sta. Esperanza
19	S. Nemesio
20	S. Julio
21	S. Pedro C.
22	S. Demetrio
23	Sta. Victoria
24	S. Delfín
25	**NATIVIDAD**
26	S. Esteban
27	S. Juan E.
28	Stos. Inocentes
29	Sto. Tomás B.
30	S. Rainerio
31	S. Silvestre

name is **Gómez**, and her mother's maiden name is **Álvarez**. If **Ana** marries **Carlos Pérez Fernández**, their child's last names will be **Pérez Gómez. Ana** herself would be **Señora Ana Gómez Álvarez de Pérez**, because women in the Hispanic world keep their maiden name after marriage. Sounds complicated? It really isn't, once you get used to it!

With the help of your teacher, find out what your name and your mother's name would be if you lived in a Spanish-speaking country.

4 *Numbers*

Rosita's clues:

$$\left.\begin{array}{l} c+e \\ c+i \end{array}\right\} = c \text{ in cent}$$

catorce, cinco

$$\left.\begin{array}{l} c+a \\ c+o \\ c+u \end{array}\right\} = c \text{ in cat}$$

catorce, Conchita, curso

You will soon be able to count to forty in Spanish. Listen to your teacher or the cassette to learn how to say the numbers 1 to 20.

1. Cover page 18 with a sheet of paper. Then cover the Spanish number words below and say the numbers aloud in Spanish.
2. Now cover the Spanish number words and write the Spanish number words in the blank lines.

catorce	_____	14	diez	_____	10
cinco	_____	5	dos	_____	2
ocho	_____	8	veinte	_____	20
diecinueve	_____	19	seis	_____	6
doce	_____	12	once	_____	11
dieciocho	_____	18	tres	_____	3
nueve	_____	9	quince	_____	15
dieciséis	_____	16	siete	_____	7
cuatro	_____	4	trece	_____	13
diecisiete	_____	17	uno	_____	1

3. Pretend you are the teacher and correct your work with a red pen or pencil. You will be able to see at a glance which words you need to study further.

ACTIVIDAD

Your teacher will read some Spanish numbers to you. Write the numerals for the number you hear:

1. _____   4. _____   7. _____   10. _____

2. _____   5. _____   8. _____   11. _____

3. _____   6. _____   9. _____   12. _____

Let's continue learning numbers. Listen to your teacher or the cassette to learn how to say the numbers 21 to 40.

Cover the top of page 20 with a sheet of paper while you do the next three activities. Your teacher will read some numbers from 21 to 40 in random order to you. Write the numerals for the Spanish number word you hear:

1. _____   6. _____

2. _____   7. _____

3. _____   8. _____

4. _____   9. _____

5. _____   10. _____

See how many Spanish number words you can recognize. Draw a line to match the Spanish number word with its numeral:

veintiséis	23
treinta y dos	34
veintitrés	36
treinta y cuatro	40
veintinueve	39
cuarenta	29
treinta y seis	32
veintiocho	21
treinta y nueve	26
veintiuno	28

Now your teacher will read some numbers in English. Write the number words in Spanish:

1. _____   6. _____

2. _____   7. _____

3. _____   8. _____

4. _____   9. _____

5. _____   10. _____

Now that you know the numbers from 1 to 40, let's try some math. First let's look at some words you will need to know:

cinco **y** ocho **son** trece

diecinueve **menos** siete **son** doce

5 + 8 = 13   19 − 7 = 12

Now write the answers to the following arithmetic problems in Spanish. Then find the correct answers in the puzzle. Circle them from left to right, right to left, up or down, or diagonally:

1. cuatro y cinco son   _____

2. once y diez y siete son   _____

3. veinticinco y catorce son   _____

4. doce y tres son   _____

5. siete y seis son   _____

6. treinta y ocho menos veintidós son   _____

7. trece y catorce son   _____

8. treinta y dos menos veinticinco son   _____

9. veintiocho menos dieciséis son   _____

10. diecinueve menos cinco son   _____

11. neuve menos seis son   _____

12. cuarenta menos cinco son   _____

13. siete menos dos son   _____.

14. diez y diez son   _____.

15. treinta y tres y siete son   _____.

16. veintitrés y siete son   _____.

17. quince y dos son   _____.

18. treinta y siete menos quince son   _____.

19. quince y cuatro son   _____.

20. diez y uno son   _____.

```
D I E C I S É I S A S P L S T
A O C N I C Y A T N I E R T S
E V E I N T I O C H O O R I E
E E Y O D I R S M E Z R E T V
T R A E C N O E T C S T I S E
E O T Q A D X N C X E S P S U
I C N H G I I N D E P Z U A N
S N E Z V E I N T I D Ó S S Y
I I R E V C S A T N I E R T A
T C A C Z I E Z Y B U R E E T
N T U R Z S L P C S Q R D V N
I Q C O D I E C I N U E V E I
E R C T N E R O G Q R T O U E
V O C A U T R A E A N E U N R
T D O C E E S I E C N I U Q T
```

5 Days of the Week

Rosita's clues:

$$g+i \atop g+e \} = \text{h in hurry}$$

jueves, Jaime, Gilberto, generación

NOVIEMBRE

lunes	martes	miércoles	jueves	viernes	sábado	domingo
1	2	3	4	5	6	7
8	9	10	11	12	13	14
15	16	17	18	19	20	21
22	23	24	25	26	27	28
29	30	31				

These are the days of the week in Spanish. The first letter is not capitalized. The Spanish week begins with Monday.

Hoy es lunes. = *Today is Monday.*

Each day, find as many people as you can and tell them the day of the week in Spanish.

Rincón cultural En la escuela (At school)

Complete the following school schedule with the subjects you are taking this year:

	LUNES	MARTES	MIERCOLES	JUEVES	VIERNES

Now look at a schedule of a Mexican middle-school student. Compare it with yours. What are the differences? What are the similarities?

	LUNES	MARTES	MIERCOLES	JUEVES	VIERNES
7:00 – 7:50	Math	Math	Math	Math	Math
8:00 – 8:50	English	English	English	English	English
9:00 – 9:50	Science	Science	Science	Science	Science
10:00 – 10:50	Social Studies	Social Studies	Social Studies	Social Studies	Social Studies
11:00 – 11:50	Spanish	Spanish	Spanish	Spanish	Spanish
1:00 – 1:50	Physical Education	Physical Education	Physical Education	Physical Education	Physical Education

As you can see, this Mexican student's school day begins and ends early. In some urban areas, where the population is very high, two school shifts exist: from 7:00 a.m. to 2:00 p.m. and from 2:00 p.m. to 8:00 p.m. In many cities, a third school shift is available for adults.

Although grading systems vary in Spanish-speaking countries, often a 10-point grading system is used — 10 being the highest grade, 1 the lowest, and 5 the passing grade. In Mexico and Puerto Rico, students' grades range from 0 to 100.

6 Months of the Year

Rosita's clues:

$g+a$
$g+o$
$g+u$ $\Big\} = g$ in gust

Margarita, agosto, gusto

The months of the year in Spanish resemble English. Can you recognize all of them? *Note:* In ordinary lowercase type, the first letter is not capitalized.

ENERO   FEBRERO   MARZO   ABRIL

MAYO   JUNIO   JULIO   AGOSTO

SEPTIEMBRE   OCTUBRE   NOVIEMBRE   DICIEMBRE

Unscramble the letters to form the name of a Spanish month:

1. T G O A O S

2. L O U I J

3. R E U C T B O

4. N E O R E

5. O M Y A

6. E M B P T S R E I E

7. Z A R M O

8. N I O U J

9. N E B M I O R E V

10. E D M R C E I I B

11. R E R F B O E

12. L I B R A

Match the names of the months with their numbers by drawing lines between the two columns. For example, January is number one and December is number twelve:

abril	nueve
agosto	dos
diciembre	diez
enero	cuatro
febrero	seis
julio	tres
junio	once
marzo	siete
mayo	uno
noviembre	ocho
octubre	doce
septiembre	cinco

ACTIVIDAD

Answer the following questions with the Spanish months:

1. In which months do you have vacation? _En_____

2. In which month is your birthday? _En_____

3. In which month does your mother celebrate her birthday? _____

4. In which month does your father celebrate his birthday? _____

5. In which month does your best friend celebrate her/his birthday? _____

6. When does your teacher celebrate her/his birthday? _____

7. Which is your favorite month? ___Es_____

8. Which is your least favorite month? _Es_____

9. In which month does your school start? _En_____

10. When do you like to play outside? ___En_____

11. When is it too cold to play outdoors? _En_____

12. What is the best month for flying kites? _Es_____

ACTIVIDAD

Fill in the blanks with the correct Spanish names of the days or months, then find the nineteen names of the day or month in the puzzle. Circle them from left to right, right to left, up or down, or diagonally:

1. The day after Monday: _____

2. The day before Thursday: _____

3. The last day of your school week: _____

4. The day before Friday: _____

5. The first day of the weekend: _____

6. Many people go to church on this day of the week: _____

7. The first day of your school week: _____

8. The month of the United States' birthday: _____

9. Labor Day occurs toward the beginning of this month: (Sept.) _____

10. New Year's Day is the first day of this month: _____

11. April Fool's Day is the first day of this month: _____

12. The month of Christmas: _____

13. Memorial Day occurs toward the end of this month: (May) _____

14. The month of Valentine's Day: _____

15. The month after July: _____

16. The month of Thanksgiving: _____

17. Halloween is on the last day of this month: _____

18. The month of St. Patrick's day: _____

19. The first month of summer: _____

```
O D A B A S N U T U E S O O E
M M A R Z O H O N B E P I C A
I D A G O S T O V V A M L T Z
C I S E L O C R E I M X U U N
O Y V O Z O G U L V E G J B S
E A R S B P J D I A I M Y R E
R O U E N E R O R L B F B E P
B I T A X I E A T J H R O R T
M N V I E R N E S I A B I I E
E U P S Q P W O X M C T O L D
I J T O R E R B E F T I Y W A
C L N P D O M I N G O S A Q P
I E R B M E I T P E S J M K L
D O X P Q L U N E S E T R A M
```

Now that you have learned the names of the days and months, let's learn how to say dates. When Spanish speakers want to say, "Today is Friday, July fourteenth," they say, **"Hoy es viernes, el catorce de julio."** "Today is Friday, March first" would be **"Hoy es viernes, el primero* de marzo."**

Your teacher will now divide the class into small groups. Each of you will choose your birthday month and make up a calendar for that month. Complete the calendar with the days of the week and the month in Spanish and enter the dates.

LUNES						DOMINGO

Now that you have completed your calendar, take turns pointing to several dates and saying them to your partners. Then point to the date of your birthdate and say: **Mi cumpleaños es** *(My birthday is)* ... followed by the date.

* Spanish uses the word **primero** instead of **uno** for the first day of the month.

Rosita's clue:

Y = ee of sheep

Y hoy, esto**y** m**u**y bien.

Diálogo 2 · *¿Qué es?*

Now let's review what you learned in Dialog 2:

1. Hola, _____ (name of friend) ¿Cómo estás?

2. Así, así. ¿Y tú?
Estoy muy bien, gracias.

3. ¿Qué es?
Es un(a) _____.

4. Muchas gracias.
De nada.

Rincón cultural   Hispanic Holidays

What is the first thing many students look for on the school calendar? Days off. Students in Spanish-speaking countries are given time off for the following holidays:

All Soul's Day (*el Día de los Muertos*): November 2. A day of remembrance of relatives and friends who have passed on.

Christmas (*Navidad*): December 25. Christmas Eve is celebrated with a mass and a big dinner afterward. Many celebrate the season by singing late night serenades to relatives and friends, who in return offer them traditional food and drinks. Students enjoy two weeks of vacation during Christmas and New Year.

Epiphany (*el Día de los Reyes Magos*): January 6. This day commemorates the visit of the three kings bearing gifts to the infant Jesus. Most Hispanic children receive presents on January 6 instead of December 25.

Good Friday *(Viernes Santo)* and **Easter** *(Pascua)* are two of the most important Hispanic holidays, when everyday life comes to a stop. People attend special masses, and thousands of devoted Christians participate in religious processions held in every city and town. Students enjoy a one-week recess during Easter.

Columbus Day *(Día de la Raza):* October 12 is a holiday in the whole Spanish-speaking world. It commemorates the discovery of the New World. On this day, people celebrate the diversity, richness, and contributions of the races and cultures that make up the Hispanic identity.

Labor Day *(Día del Trabajo)* is celebrated on May 1, except in Puerto Rico, where the American tradition is followed.

Every Spanish American country has its own national holiday to commemorate important dates in its struggle for independence from Spain. For example, in Mexico, it's September 16; in Colombia, July 20; in Chile, September 18; in the Dominican Republic, February 27.

Each country also has holidays that commemorate other special historical events, such as May 5 in Mexico, which commemorates a victory against the French invasion in the nineteenth century, or November 19 in Puerto Rico, the day the island was discovered.

1. When do Hispanic children generally receive Christmas presents?

_____

2. How long is Easter break in Hispanic countries?

_____

3. What does the Spanish-speaking world celebrate on Columbus Day?

7 The Classroom

h is not pronounced in Spanish.

ɦola, ɦoy, ɦoja

qui=ki in ski
que=ka in skate

quince, ¿Qué es?

Learn the names of the objects in your classroom. See how many you can remember at a time without having to look at the book:

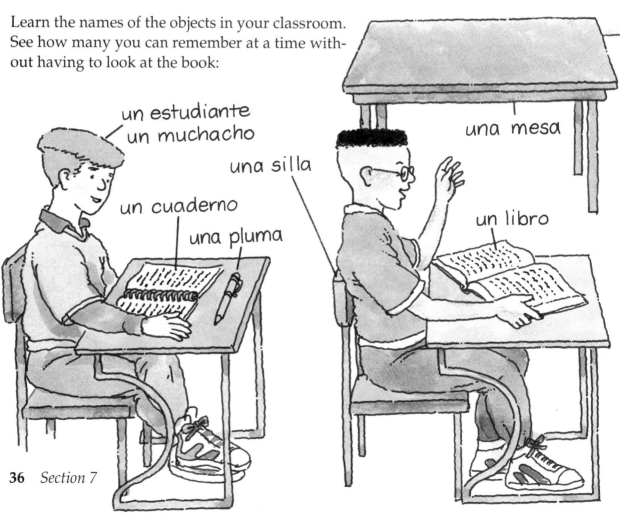

un estudiante
un muchacho

una silla

un cuaderno

una pluma

una mesa

un libro

una pizarra

una ventana

una profesora

un pedazo de tiza

un profesor

una puerta   una hoja de papel

una estudiante
una muchacha

un pupitre

un lápiz

un escritorio

In Spanish, every noun is considered masculine or feminine. The masculine indefinite article (*a, an*) is **un** and the feminine is **una**.

1. Name aloud as many of the classroom words in Spanish as you can remember. Study the words you did not remember.

2. Write the name of the illustrations in Spanish in the first column of blank lines.

3. Correct your work. Give yourself one point for each correct answer.

4. Now cover the illustrations and write the English meanings of the Spanish words in the second column of blank lines.

5. Correct your work. Give yourself one point for each correct answer.

WRITE SPANISH WORDS HERE   WRITE ENGLISH WORDS HERE

1. _____   _____

2. _____   _____

3. _____   _____

4. _____   _____

5. _____   _____

6. _____   _____

7. _____ _____

8. _____ _____

9. _____ _____

10. _____ _____

11. _____ _____

12. _____ _____

13. _____ _____

14. _____ _____

15. _____ _____

16. _____ _____

17. _____ _____

Thirty-four points is a perfect score. If you made a mistake, you can improve your score by repeating the exercise on a blank piece of paper and correcting it again.

Classroom Vocabulary Puzzle: To solve this puzzle, first express the following words in Spanish then fit them in the puzzle vertically and horizontally:

4-letter words

table ___ ___ ___ ___

chalk ___ ___ ___ ___

5-letter words

book ___ ___ ___ ___ ___

paper ___ ___ ___ ___ ___

pencil ___ ___ ___ ___ ___

chair ___ ___ ___ ___ ___

pen ___ ___ ___ ___ ___

6-letter word

door ___ ___ ___ ___ ___ ___

7-letter words

chalkboard ___ ___ ___ ___ ___ ___ ___

window ___ ___ ___ ___ ___ ___ ___

8-letter words

boy ___ ___ ___ ___ ___ ___ ___ ___

girl ___ ___ ___ ___ ___ ___ ___ ___

notebook ___ ___ ___ ___ ___ ___ ___ ___

9-letter word

female teacher ___ ___ ___ ___ ___ ___ ___ ___ ___

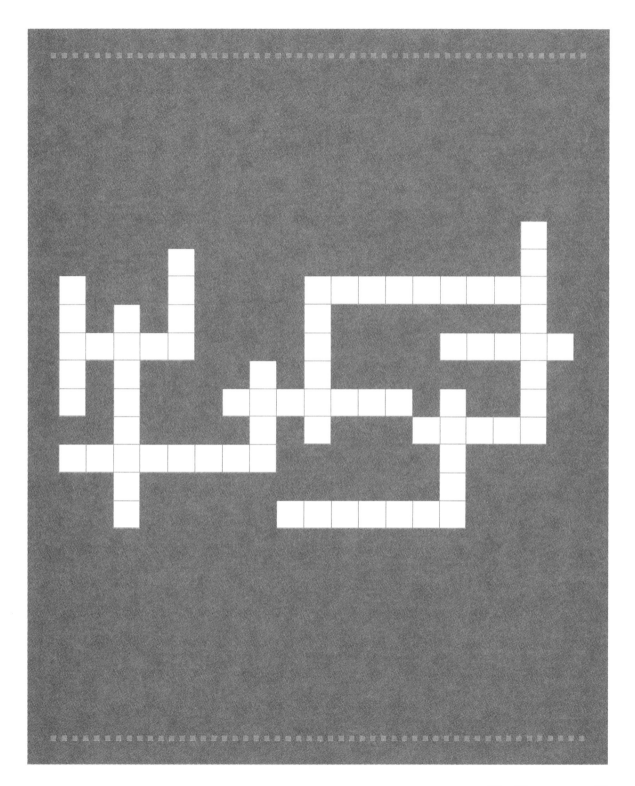

Hispanic children spend their free time in a variety of activities with family and friends. Because Hispanic schools normally do not sponsor activities like sports, dances, or games, most students go to youth centers or clubs to take classes in areas of interest ranging from music, dance, arts and crafts, to sports, martial arts, computer science, and foreign languages.

Hispanic teens like to go out in groups. Teenagers with similar backgrounds or from the same school tend to form a special group of close friends who meets regularly to chat at cafés, take walks, go dancing, and have parties. Even when teenagers date, usually beginning at the age of 16, it is still uncommon for a couple to go out alone unless the relationship is more serious.

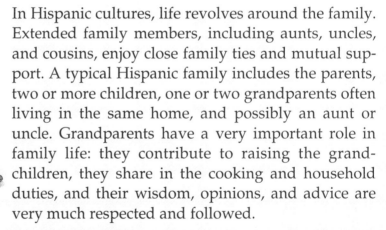

In Hispanic cultures, life revolves around the family. Extended family members, including aunts, uncles, and cousins, enjoy close family ties and mutual support. A typical Hispanic family includes the parents, two or more children, one or two grandparents often living in the same home, and possibly an aunt or uncle. Grandparents have a very important role in family life: they contribute to raising the grandchildren, they share in the cooking and household duties, and their wisdom, opinions, and advice are very much respected and followed.

Meals are an important time for the family to gather, eat leisurely, and engage in lively conversation. Stores and offices generally close from noon to two o'clock in order to give workers time to go home and have a traditional midday meal with the family. If time allows, an afternoon siesta or nap is enjoyed before returning to work. The practice of extended midday breaks has been gradually disappearing in the large cities.

Do your grandparents live with you? _____

What is a siesta? _____

8 | *Colors*

Rosita's clues:

ll = y in yes*

me **ll**amo, si**ll**a, amari**ll**o

rr = sound of a motorcycle motor
r = dd in ladder

ma**rr**ón, guita**rr**a   mo**r**ado, amarillo

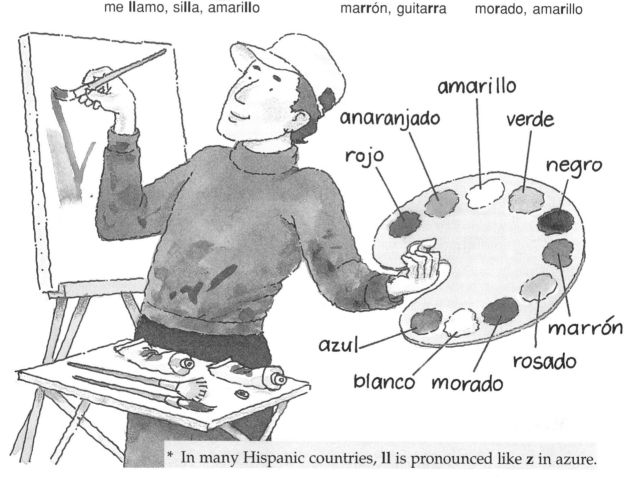

anaranjado

amarillo

rojo

verde

negro

azul

blanco morado

rosado

marrón

* In many Hispanic countries, **ll** is pronounced like **z** in azure.

How many of the Spanish color words can you memorize in one minute? Two minutes? Five? When you feel ready, test yourself:

1. Say as many Spanish color words as you can remember.
2. Write the Spanish color words in the first column of blank lines.
3. Check your work and give yourself one point for each correct answer.
4. Now cover the colors and write the English meanings of the Spanish color words in the second column of blank lines.
5. Check your work and give yourself one point for each correct answer.

WRITE SPANISH WORDS HERE   WRITE ENGLISH WORDS HERE

1. _____   _____

2. _____   _____

3. _____   _____

4. _____   _____

5. _____   _____

6. _____   _____

7. _____   _____

8. _____   _____

9. _____   _____

10. _____   _____

Did you get 20 points? If not, try again with a blank piece of paper.

Here are pictures of items you have already learned:

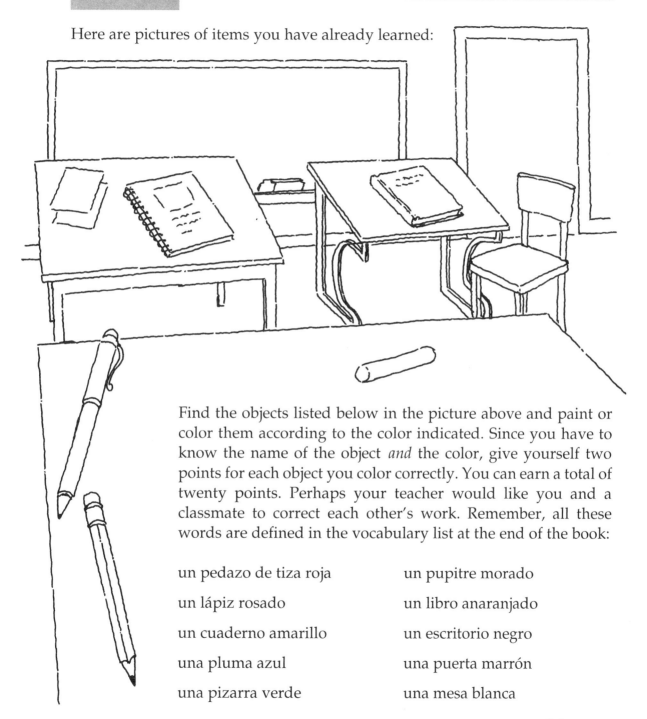

Find the objects listed below in the picture above and paint or color them according to the color indicated. Since you have to know the name of the object *and* the color, give yourself two points for each object you color correctly. You can earn a total of twenty points. Perhaps your teacher would like you and a classmate to correct each other's work. Remember, all these words are defined in the vocabulary list at the end of the book:

un pedazo de tiza roja	un pupitre morado
un lápiz rosado	un libro anaranjado
un cuaderno amarillo	un escritorio negro
una pluma azul	una puerta marrón
una pizarra verde	una mesa blanca

You have already seen this map of the world. Color all the countries where Spanish is spoken. Color the countries in each continent according to the colors below:

Europe — **amarillo**

South America — **rojo**

Central America — **azul**

North America — **verde**

Island Countries — **anaranjado**

9 *The Body*

Rosita's clue:

ñ = ny in canyon

español, señor, señorita

la cabeza

el ojo

la nariz

la boca

la mano

la oreja

el brazo

la pierna

el pie

When you want to talk about yourself in Spanish, you will need to know the names of the parts of the body. How many names can you remember without having to look at the book?

You have already learned that the masculine article **un** and the feminine article **una** mean *a, an*. Now let's learn how to express English *the*. Did you notice the words **el** and **la** before all of the nouns? To say *the*, Spanish uses **el** before masculine nouns and **la** before feminine nouns.

Fill in the names of the parts of the body:

Choose a partner. Point to each other's hand, foot, and so on, and ask, **"¿Qué es?"** Answer, **"Es una mano." "Es un pie."** And so on.

Complete this crossword puzzle with the
Spanish names of the parts of the body:

Across   **Down**

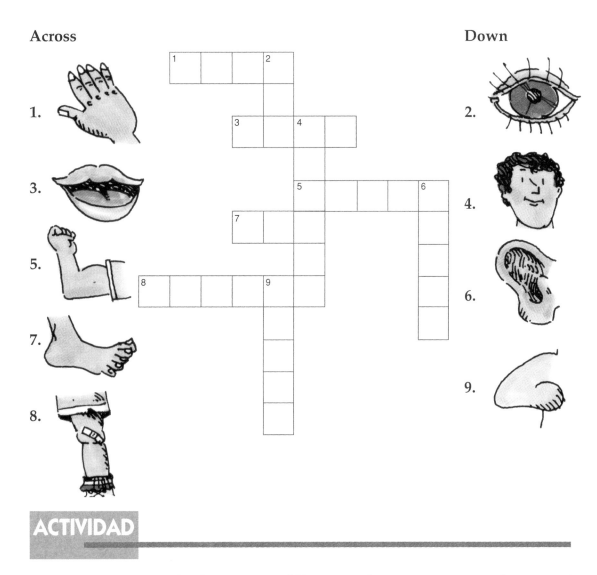

1.   2.

3.   4.

5.   6.

7.

8.   9.

"Simón dice" means *"Simon says."* Move or point to that part of
the body Simon refers to only if you hear the words **"Simón dice."**
If you do not hear the words **"Simón dice,"** don't move at all.

Rincón cultural

Some Interesting Manners and Customs

People of Spanish heritage tend to be very affectionate with family and friends and warm when meeting new people. They readily express their feelings and have more physical contact than Americans. It is common practice for women friends as well as friends of the opposite sex to kiss each other when meeting and again when parting. Men generally greet with a handshake, a pat on the back, and occasionally an embrace. Unlike most Americans, who put a high premium on personal space and privacy, Hispanics enjoy being physically close with their friends. It is not unusual to touch a friend's arm, hand, or leg during conversation, to walk arm in arm, and for younger female friends to hold hands.

In the United States, a formal invitation to dinner is usually necessary. In Spain and Spanish America by contrast, friends will often pop in unexpectedly at mealtime and are automatically invited to share the meal.

People from Spanish-speaking countries differ from Americans not only in what they eat but also in when they eat. Breakfast is served between seven and nine o'clock and is usually light, consisting of fritters, toast, coffee with or without milk, or hot chocolate. Lunch, the biggest meal of the day is served between noon and two o'clock. Supper, generally a light meal, is not eaten earlier than 7:00 p.m. and often not until nine or ten o'clock at night. At the beginning of a meal, it is customary for everyone at the table to say **"¡Buen provecho!"** (*"Enjoy the meal!"*)

Americans are sometimes puzzled when they observe people from Spanish-speaking countries during mealtime because they hold the fork in the left hand and the knife in the right, keeping them this way throughout the meal, even after cutting their food. The knife is not put down while eating and the fork does not change hands.

Would you be confused if you opened a Spanish television guide and saw listed programs starting at 18:00, 22:00, or 00:30 o'clock? Spanish-speaking countries use the 24-hour system for official time — schedules for planes, trains, radio and television programs, movies, sports events, and so on. With this system, they avoid confusion as well as the need to use a.m. or p.m.

CONVENTIONAL TIME	OFFICIAL TIME
8:00 a.m.	08,00 **(a las ocho)**
noon	12,00 **(a las doce)**
2:00 p.m.	14,00 **(a las catorce)**
6 p.m.	18,00 **(a las diez y ocho)**
midnight	24,00 **(a las veinte y cuatro)**
12:15 a.m.	00,15 **(a las cero y quince)**

Note: In Hispanic countries, a comma is used in numbers expressing time instead of a colon.

To calculate official time, add 12 to the conventional time for the hours between noon and midnight.

8:00 a.m.	08,00
8:00 p.m.	20,00

10 Talking About Yourself

An adjective describes a person or thing. In the sentence "The beautiful girl is happy," *beautiful* and *happy* are adjectives that describe *girl*. Many adjectives are easy to remember if you think of them in pairs:

delgado	**gordo**	**inteligente**	**tonto**
triste	**alegre**	**pequeño**	**grande**
guapo	**feo**	**fuerte**	**débil**

Cover page 52 with a sheet of paper and write the Spanish adjectives that describe the objects you see:

1. _____

2. _____

3. _____

4. _____

5. _____

6. _____

7. _____

8. _____

9. _____

10. _____

11. _____

12. _____

Diálogo 3   *Yo estoy . . . / Yo soy . . .*

* Note that Spanish speakers commonly omit **yo** and **tú** before the verb.

In Dialog 3, you may have noticed that Spanish has two ways of saying *I am*: **yo estoy** and **yo soy**. Let's compare the difference between these two verbs.

estoy is used to describe how you feel at the moment you are speaking:

Yo estoy alegre. *I am happy.*

Yo estoy triste. *I am sad.*

soy is used to describe what kind of person you are all the time:

Yo soy inteligente. *I am intelligent.*

Yo soy guapo. *I am good-looking.*

Look at these pictures. Can you explain why the girl uses **yo estoy** and the boy uses **yo soy**?

When you want to say *you are*, choose between **tú estás** and **tú eres:**

Tú estás alegre.   Tú eres inteligente.

To say *he is* choose between **él está** and **él es;** and to say *she is* choose between **ella está** and **ella es.**

Él / Ella está triste.   Él / Ella es fuerte.

Now it's your turn. Can you complete what the young people in these pictures are saying? Use one of the verbs on page 56.

1.

2.

3.

4.

Let's learn some more about adjectives. Look at the adjectives on the left that could describe a boy. Compare them with the adjectives on the right that could describe a girl:

delgado	delgada
gordo	gorda
tonto	tonta
guapo	guapa
feo	fea
pequeño	pequeña

Spanish adjectives, like nouns, have a gender. A feminine adjective is used to describe a feminine noun and a masculine adjective is used to describe a masculine noun. Which letter do we change in the masculine adjective to get the feminine?

ACTIVIDAD

Use as many of the adjectives above to describe these animals:

_____   _____

_____   _____

_____   _____

_____   _____

ACTIVIDAD

You have already learned that changing the final **o** of a Spanish adjective to **a** gives you the feminine form. Now let's learn about the feminine forms of other adjectives.

Adjectives that do not end in **o** — like **alegre, triste, inteligente, fuerte, grande,** and **débil** — do not change in the feminine. Isn't that easy?

Let's practice these adjectives by filling in the blanks with the adjective that describes the people in the pictures:

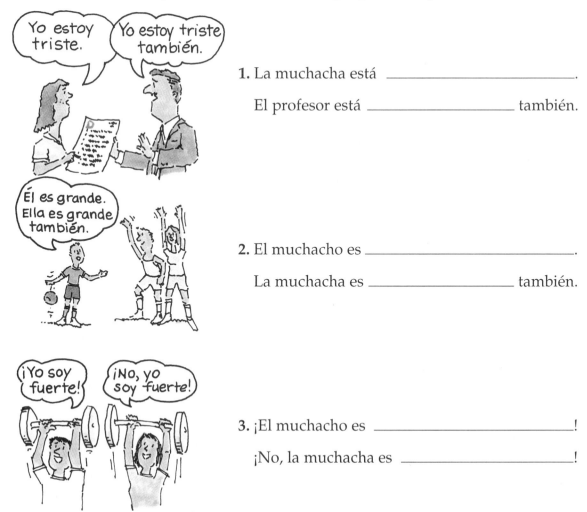

1. La muchacha está _____.

   El profesor está _____ también.

2. El muchacho es _____.

   La muchacha es _____ también.

3. ¡El muchacho es _____!

   ¡No, la muchacha es _____!

Talking About Yourself **59**

1. How many of the boys in this basketball team can you describe? Write the adjective that best describes each player next to his number in the column of blank lines:

MUCHACHOS

1 _____

2 _____

3 _____

4 _____

5 _____

6 _____

7 _____

8 _____

9 _____

10 _____

2. How would you change the adjectives to describe each player of the opposing girls' team? Write the adjective that best describes each player next to her number in the column of blank lines:

MUCHACHAS

1 _____
2 _____
3 _____
4 _____
5 _____
6 _____
7 _____
8 _____
9 _____
10 _____

ACTIVIDAD

Your teacher will now divide you into small groups to practice describing yourself and one another.

ACTIVIDAD

Play charades with the adjectives you have learned. Your teacher will divide the class into teams, and a member from one team will stand in front of the class and act out the various ways he or she would look if sad, intelligent, fat, and so on.

Rincón cultural

Los deportes (Sports)

In Spain and Spanish America, soccer **(fútbol)** is a passion bordering on obsession. Most large and small cities have their own teams. Many different types of soccer teams are popular: neighborhood teams, company teams, soccer club teams, as well as professional teams. National games are very important and the competition is fierce. International soccer competitions are occasions for great patriotic enthusiasm, and soccer teams are revered as national symbols. In almost every park and empty lot in every town, boys of all ages can be seen playing soccer and dreaming of becoming the next international soccer star.

What is less known is that other sports, like baseball, are also becoming more and more popular in many Hispanic countries. In the Caribbean, in Cuba, the Dominican Republic, Puerto Rico, Mexico, Nicaragua, and Venezuela, baseball is extremely important. Many famous major league baseball players in the United States have come from Cuba, the Dominican Republic, and Puerto Rico.

Cycling is very important in Spain, Colombia, Mexico, Cuba, Chile, and Costa Rica. Each country has its national race once a year that lasts a couple of weeks. The winner is a national hero.

There is also a lesser known, very ancient sport, **jai-alai**, which has its origins in the Basque region of Spain. It's probably the fastest game in the world. Played with a hard ball and a wicker basket strapped to the wrist on a court with high walls, **jai-alai** resembles handball, except for the basket. This sport is popular in Spain, Cuba, Mexico, and Venezuela, as well as in Florida and Connecticut.

Spain as well as some Spanish-American countries, especially Mexico and Colombia, are also known for bullfighting (**corridas de toro**).

1. What is the Spanish word for soccer? _____

_____

2. Would you be interested in seeing a bullfight? _____

_____

11 *Recycling Spanish*

Your teacher will now give you time to use your Spanish. Think of all you have learned!

- You can say your name!
- You can count and do math!
- You can name the days of the week and the months of the year!
- You can name objects in the classroom with their colors!
- You can describe yourself and others and point out parts of the body!

When someone asks if you speak Spanish: **¿Hablas español?**, now you can answer: **¡Sí, hablo español!**

ACTIVIDAD

Fill in the boxes with the Spanish meanings and you will find a mystery word in the longest vertical column. Write the mystery word in Spanish and English in the blanks provided:

1. head
2. Good-bye.
3. October
4. Miss
5. ten
6. sad
7. Sunday
8. yellow
9. fifteen
10. Hello.

Colors: What would this funny monster look like if you could color the parts of its body? Write the names of the parts of the body and colors you would choose in the blanks below. Then color the parts of the body in the picture:

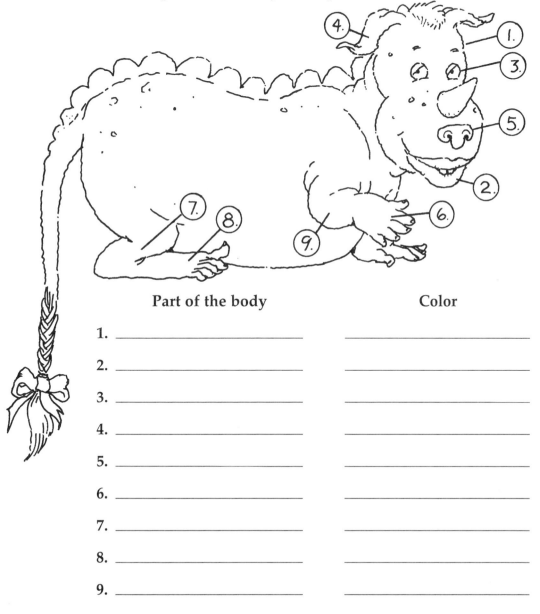

Part of the body	Color
1. _____	_____
2. _____	_____
3. _____	_____
4. _____	_____
5. _____	_____
6. _____	_____
7. _____	_____
8. _____	_____
9. _____	_____

Can you complete these dialogs or express the following ideas in Spanish?

1. You overhear the conversation of these two people, who are meeting for the first time. Complete the dialog:

2. Peter is teaching some Spanish words to his little brother. Complete the dialog:

3. What do you think these friends are saying to each other?

4. What are the colors of the Mexican flag?

_____   _____   _____

5. What are the names of these parts of the body?

 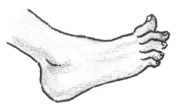 

_____   _____   _____

6. What days of the week are missing from this agenda?

Enero
9 lunes
10
11 miércoles
12
13 viernes
14
15

7. What month is it?

_____   _____   _____

8. What adjectives describe these people?

_____   _____   _____

ACTIVIDAD

Tómbola is played like Bingo, except that our **Tómbola** is played with words. Select Spanish words from categories in the vocabulary list on pages 72 to 74 as directed by your teacher. Write one word across each square at random from the chosen categories.

Your teacher will read the **Tómbola** words in English. If one of the Spanish words on your card matches the English word you hear, mark that square with a small star. When you have five stars in a row, either horizontally, vertically, or diagonally, call out, **"¡Gané!"** (*"I won!"*)

Rincón cultural

¡Vivan las diferencias! (Hurrah for the differences!)

Now that you have learned quite a bit about the Spanish language
and about the Spanish-speaking world and its people, can you list
the differences that impressed you most between Hispanic and American people. Jog your memory by looking over cultural pages 16–17,
25, 34–35, 42, 50–51, and 62–63.

An example is given to get you started:

	SPANISH	AMERICAN
1.	*Each person uses the father's last name plus the mother's maiden name.*	*Only one family name is used: the father's last name.*
2.		
3.		
4.		
5.		
6.		

Vocabulary

Numbers

uno	1
dos	2
tres	3
cuatro	4
cinco	5
seis	6
siete	7
ocho	8
nueve	9
diez	10
once	11
doce	12
trece	13
catorce	14
quince	15
dieciséis	16
diecisiete	17
dieciocho	18
diecinueve	19
veinte	20
veintiuno	21
veintidós	22
veintitrés	23
veinticuatro	24
veinticinco	25
veintiséis	26
veintisiete	27
veintiocho	28
veintinueve	29
treinta	30
treinta y uno	31
treinta y dos	32
treinta y tres	33
treinta y cuatro	34
treinta y cinco	35
treinta y seis	36
treinta y siete	37
treinta y ocho	38
treinta y nueve	39
cuarenta	40

Arithmetic

¿Cuántos?	How many?
y	plus
menos	minus
son	are, equal

Days of the week

lunes	Monday
martes	Tuesday
miércoles	Wednesday
jueves	Thursday
viernes	Friday
sábado	Saturday
domingo	Sunday

Months of the year

enero	January
febrero	February
marzo	March
abril	April
mayo	May
junio	June
julio	July
agosto	August
septiembre	September
octubre	October
noviembre	November
diciembre	December

The Classroom

un cuaderno	a notebook
un escritorio	a teacher's desk
un(a) estudiante	a student
una hoja de papel	a piece of paper
un lápiz	a pencil
un libro	a book
una mesa	a table
una muchacha	a girl
un muchacho	a boy
una pizarra	a chalkboard
una pluma	a pen
un profesor	a male teacher
una profesora	a female teacher
una puerta	a door
un pupitre	a student's desk
un pedazo de tiza	a piece of chalk
un profesor	a male teacher
una profesora	a female teacher
una silla	a chair
una ventana	a window

Colors

amarillo, amarilla	yellow
anaranjado, anaranjada	orange
azul	blue
blanco, blanca	white
morado, morada	purple
marrón	brown
negro, negra	black
rojo, roja	red
rosado, rosada	pink
verde	green

The Body

la boca	the mouth
el brazo	the arm
la cabeza	the head
la mano	the hand
la nariz	the nose
el ojo	the eye
la oreja	the ear
el pie	the foot
la pierna	the leg

Adjectives

alegre	happy
débil	weak
delgado, delgada	thin
feo, fea	ugly
fuerte	strong
gordo, gorda	fat
grande	tall, big
guapo, guapa	beautiful, handsome
inteligente	intelligent
pequeño, pequeña	small, short
tonto, tonta	stupid
triste	sad

Expressions and phrases

Buenos días.	Good morning.
Adiós.	Good-bye.
¡Hola!	Hello! / Hi!
¿Cómo te llamas?	What's your name?
Me llamo . . .	My name is . . .
¿Y tú?	And you?
Mucho gusto.	Pleased to meet you.
El gusto es mío.	The pleasure is mine.
¿Cómo estás?	How are you?
Estoy muy bien.	I am very well.
Así, así.	So, so.
¿Qué es?	What is it?
¿Cuántos?	How many?
Es un (una) . . .	It is a . . .
Para ti.	For you.

Gracias.	Thank you.
Muchas gracias.	Thank you very much.
De nada.	You're welcome.
Yo estoy . . .	I am . . .
Tú estás . . .	You are . . .
Ella / Él está . . .	She / He is . . .
La muchacha está . . .	The girl is . . .
El muchacho está . . .	The boy is . . .
Yo soy . . .	I am . . .
Tú eres . . .	You are . . .
Ella / Él es . . .	She / He is . . .
La muchacha es . . .	The girl is . . .
El muchacho es . . .	The boy is . . .
Hoy es . . .	Today is . . .
Lo siento.	I'm sorry.
Por favor.	Please.
¿Por qué?	Why?
porque	because
y	and
muy	very
ahora	now
también	also
Sí.	Yes.
No.	No.
señor	Mister, sir
señora	Mrs., madame
señorita	Miss
Rincón cultural	Cultural corner